READ ME BiTCH (THiS iS

READ ME BiTCH (THiS iS WHAT iT MEANS TO BE HUMAN)

Dear Reader,

I feel like I need to explain myself, a little, to you before you embark upon this mind-fuck through my thoughts and feelings over the last 5 years. But if I do that you don't get to come to your own conclusions…so…

With that said, I hope my words touch your soul in some tiny way…

Happy Reading

Sincerely,

Meghanne Storey
Singer/Songwriter/Poet

PS The pictures below are of my project and my brothers and nephew, who have passed on, but I chose to remember them in some of these rhymes.

READ ME BiTCH (THiS iS WHAT iT MEANS TO BE HUMAN)

Jesse See

Mark Storey

READ ME BiTCH (THiS iS WHAT iT MEANS TO BE HUMAN)

**The Meghanne Storey Project
Busking at Enumclaw Music Store**

READ ME BiTCH (THiS iS WHAT iT MEANS TO BE HUMAN)

Pat Storey

READ ME BiTCH (THiS iS WHAT iT MEANS TO BE HUMAN)

**The Meghanne Storey Project
#AndBuck**

READ ME BITCH:
This is what it means to be human

...a collection of writings by Meghanne Storey

Table of Contents

1. What it Means to Be Human......11
2. Empty Spaces............12
3. Questions...................12
4. Facebook Comments......13
5. Damn Shame...............14
6. Fear........................14
7. Waves and Tides..........15
8. Anchor.....................16
9. Change....................16
10. Irene......................17
11. Would You Miss Me?......19
12. The Deep Dark............19
13. Review Mirror............20
14. What a Waste.............21
15. She is.....................21
16. The Limb.................22
17. Simple Act of Kindness...22
18. With or Without You......22
19. Organized Thoughts......23
20. Guilt Free Cake.........24
21. I Remember the Love.....24
22. Blurry Days................25
23. The Fire...................26
24. Walls.....................26
25. Social Suicide............27
26. Narcissist.................28
27. Goodbye..................28
28. Untitled..................29
29. Fix Your Picker...........29
30. And I Wonder............30
31. Insomnia..................39
32. Thought and Prayers......31
33. Shady Mother Fuckers....31
34. Cash it in.................32
35. Catch and Release......32
36. Dreams..................32
37. Bliss......................33
38. Maybe it's Real............33
39. Girl.........................33
40. You Instead................35
41. Distrust....................36
42. Integrity....................36
43. Over.......................38
44. In the Afterwards..........39
45. Petrichor..................40
46. Secrets...................40
47. Thoughtful Answers.......42
48. Nightmares................43
49. The Trap...................43
50. Music is The Only Thing...44
51. Younger Ways............45
52. Something That I Said....46
53. Lost Boy (Jesse).........46
54. The Burn................47
55. THink Before You Act.....48
56. The Heart of June........48
57. Her Dream..............49
58. Unrequited..............50
59. Creepy Night-Time Sounds...52
60. The Nature of Death......53
61. Reaching Out............54
62. Waiting for Patience to Pay...55
63. Friendly Connection......56
64. Sleep Evades Me.........56
65. Wild Woman.............57

READ ME BiTCH (THiS iS WHAT iT MEANS TO BE HUMAN)

66. Smoke and Music Notes………..58
67. Heart-Shaped Faces……………59
68. Big Old Bones………………………..60
69. Little Crumbs………………………62
70. Perception…………………63
71. Little Keys…………………64
72. Scream………………………64
73. Mud Puddles……………………65
74. Messages in Bubbles……………66
75. After-Thoughts………………68
76. Strong Ass Bitch…………………69
77. Desire……………………………69
78. The Circle……………………………70
79. Let The People Go………………....70
80. Today, I Need to Write……………71
81. Tangible Flow………………………72
82. Profound…………………………72
83. I wish…………………………….73
84. Legacy………………………73
85. Fuck you……………………………..74
86. Walk Away (the end)…………………75
87. (Credits)……………………………76

Thank you

This book is dedicated to Deanna Levitt, to my brothers Mark and Pat, to my nephew Jesse, and to my children, Eliana, Daniel and Cloudy Sky. Thank you, Deanna, for being the motivation I needed to finally get this published. Thank you to my children for always reminding me that I am the only thing standing in my way.

I would also like to take a moment and acknowledge those of you who have given me so much to write about. You know who you are.

READ ME BiTCH (THiS iS WHAT iT MEANS TO BE HUMAN)

What it Means to be Human

It's what it means to be human
The struggles in your mind
Those frustrations that you find
Yeah…they give this life--specific meaning

They help create a place
A quiet, simple space
Where one can gaze into the past
And kick their own stupid ass
For all those dumb mistakes they made
And then live for a moment in the memories

It's what it means to be human
When that fire starts burning deep in your chest
And the butterflies leave imaginary nests
Beating their wings deep in your core
Causing you to always want more
And next that moment comes
And you feel like you've found the one
the fireworks from up above

Then your heart breaks
And your stomach starts to ache
And time stands still; never moving, not quite real
And you know…this is what it means to be human

The spinning around and the falling to the ground and the laughter
And never fearing what comes after
Then hitting the cement
Where time and space lament
it's what it means to be human

The questions and the answers
The curiosity that dances
Through our heads when we are young
The beauty of the world; and the ugliness of blood
All the highs and lows
When it all hurts and when you glow
This is what it means to be human.

Empty Spaces

I feel so sad
It's like you're not looking back
Like maybe you just don't see me
Or maybe this wasn't meant to be
I feel this giant hole
Where something is supposed to go
I thought that it was you
But now I feel a different hue
Colors swirling all around
My feet lift up off the ground
Like this cannot be imagined
I know it really happened
And here I sit alone in my thoughts
Wishing you were in this spot
The empty one here next to me
But it wasn't meant to be

Questions

I see him there with the wind in his hair trying to catch my eye with his stare
And I don't care...because he isn't you.
And there's another dude

READ ME BiTCH (THiS iS WHAT iT MEANS TO BE HUMAN)

Who's always coming through...he wants to make me smile too
But he can't...because he isn't you
And this other guy would like to try
...some feeling...but it won't happen...he just wants to be my captain

...what it is about you...why are you stuck in my view?
Why can't I get past you? What is it you do?

I'm so stuck in this spot...like a fish that's been caught
and I'll never get laid with this game that we play
and I'm ready for that...I want it...today!

Do you want to see if between you and me something could grow?
Because I'm at the point where I want to know.
Either that or I really have to go.

Facebook Comments

Where did all the time go?
How come no one seems to know…
No one seems to be around..
it's like they all just left and found…
Other lives to lead…
And maybe they forgot me?
How come no one ever told…
Me when I'd grow up; gray and old...
I would miss how it used to be...
I would miss that little me...
I would miss my life...
And the hard core strife...

READ ME BiTCH (THiS iS WHAT iT MEANS TO BE HUMAN)

I had to endure...
Though friends I had were the best cure…
I wish that I could find a way
To get back to those special days...
Where people gathered in a certain space...
When my life made fucking sense...
Before the facebook comments.

Damn Shame

It's a damn shame...
That you treated her that way...
She would have been your ride or die...
She was always there right by your side...
But you left her by herself...
You left her for something else...
You chose to throw your life away...
You pulled her with you as you sank...
And all that she could do was pray that someday you would go away...

Fear

It's a heavy feeling that fills the air
Like that smokey, creepy, old man stare
Like the feeling you get when you know they're there
And you might, just maybe, feel scared

It's that moment when you know it's coming
A swift blade; you can hear it humming
But it doesn't cut
Instead
It whispers secrets deep in your head

READ ME BiTCH (THiS iS WHAT iT MEANS TO BE HUMAN)

Like "there are monsters underneath your bed"

And you can't stop the madness
You can't seem to just get past it
You smell the smell of burnt up plastic
And feel the intensity of their sadness
Filling up your basket
Until it overflows
And you can't take it anymore
So you run away screaming
And all the while
      ...That's what they were...

      ...Scheming.

Waves and Tides
When I see that ocean...so blue...
And I'm so breath-taken by the view...
I step in the water and stumble and falter…
But…
I am under control...
...and you softly whisper into my ear…
Those sweet nothings, you know, I need to hear...
As your lips meet mine...the waves begin to climb…
Higher and higher…
Like the flames of a fire…
And I fall and then rise...on the waves and the tides...riding high...
    On the ocean of you...

Anchor

Oh you're mad
Of course, I knew that
Your rage is in your face
And that smile that you fake.

Do you hide inside that anger? Let it take you?
Is it your manager?
Do you let it take control
And tell you where to go
And how others see and feel your soul?

Maybe you should check your shit
Make your anger wait a bit
i don't want to tune you out but i need you to learn about
Those things that you don't understand
Those things that actually make you a man
A real man controls his anger
He doesn't let it become his anchor.

Change

As I walk through this rain
And things just stay the same
I realize I need to change

Life…she always seems to say
I just can't have these things my way
She says…

    …"you can love him but he won't stay…"

READ ME BiTCH (THiS iS WHAT iT MEANS TO BE HUMAN)

Only memories remain...
And while I cherish those I need to change

I need nothing to stay--not the letters in my name or the simple day to day

Well, some things can stay the same;
                …I think it's me who needs to change.

Irene

She called me that night to tell me about her flight
And how beautiful it was on that island paradise
But she told me one more thing
And it still fucking stings
it still fucking rings
Deep in my ears--it still fucking fills me with so much fucking fear
And i still fucking feel those stupid fucking tears
Falling on my cheeks as she said she loved me.

    …but her time has run out…

There's no stopping it now
And it hit me...like a rock...deep in my gut
And I really don't know how to handle this...FUCK...
I really don't know how to process this one.

She says she's far down that rabbit hole now
And that she is not sure she will ever climb out
There's a mass in her lung...ground glass in her lungs
And her heart's on the edge...not trying to run

READ ME BiTCH (THiS iS WHAT iT MEANS TO BE HUMAN)

And she is stuck somewhere deep in her head
Cuz she knows she is standing at the edge of that ledge
And she is struggling so hard.

She says this is the part...she iS trying to change but it's hard
To change lanes so late in the game and she isn't sure that she wants to change
Because it is HER life and she lives it this way.

So I have to just stay...and I have to just wait…
And I'll have to pray...and make sure that she knows--I love her…
Every day…anyway.

I just hope…
When she goes away...
Is far out **enough**...
That there will be time **enough**...
For her to know her grandkids…
And they can maybe have memories
        …of all the special things they did...

Would You Miss Me?

If I disappeared would I be missed?
Would my soul be one lifted into the mist?
Would people be sad if I disappeared?
Would they know that I cared before I left here?

The world will keep turning and moving through space…
Whether or not I am here holding my place…
But things would be different somehow I'm sure...

Or would I disappear quickly; my life, flash by in a blurb...

Or would the space in my chair still be there?
Would my loved ones still feel the love that I shared?
Would my memory live on?
Long after I'm gone?
Would the wind whisper the words of my last dying song?

If I disappear...say it's my time...
Did anyone miss me?
When my light ceased to shine?

The Deep Dark

In a moment you find yourself…in the deep dark
Not able to locate your...broken parts
It is then when you learn the delicate art

Of filling in holes where things used to go
And sewing on buttons to close up new holes

You can't let yourself fall apart
Even when you're lost in the deep dark
Hold your high
Someone will find
A way to get to your mark
Then..in the end…you will know how it starts
'Cause you were lost and found in the deepest of the dark.

Rear-View Mirror (Pat's Song)

Did you know your stars shine in the same sky as mine?
After the clouds drift away
Those stars light my way
On this path I travel through life?

Even though I'll never know you, touch you, feel you...
    ...or hold you...

I still know the darkness in your eyes
And the intimate way they lie

Even though you left long ago,
I can still feel you come and go.
And the way your spirit flows

    …from this realm to the next...

Sometimes when I dream at night
I wake up with a sudden bite
Something was here with me
But all I see
Are my fingers grasping at tendrils of smoke

    ...and music notes...

As you disappear...

    …into my rear-view mirror.

READ ME BiTCH (THiS iS WHAT iT MEANS TO BE HUMAN)

What a Waste
Oh my FUCKiNG GOD i CANT WiTH YOU
Because you never do what you say you're going to
Its like this stupid game
Where I say your name
And you say "no way
I never said I would make it today"
And it makes me want to scream back that you said you'd DO THAT
But i dont...I just fix it...then I sit back, no bitchin'
It's pointless for me to engage with you
Because you never do what you say you're going to.

She is...
She is wild and free
as bright as the sun
and she beats to the beat of her very own drum
she has stars in her eyes...her dreams end in sighs
             ...and she wishes she didn't always have to
       be on the run

But she has secrets she cannot impart...secrets that would tear everything apart
Any house that she builds....and all her flowers would just wilt
So she tries to be kind hearted
             ...and always finish what she's
       started...

The Limb

I put myself out as far on the limb
As I'm willing to go to try and reach him
If he doesn't get it well that's just how it is
Maybe I just wasn't meant to be his
…it's not because of his car or his clothes
It's not just because he goes with the flow
It has more to do with what's deep in his soul
That's the man I've been getting to know
But I think I went too far on that limb
…and now I think I may have lost him.

Simple Act of Kindness

It's a simple act of kindness
Proof of open mindedness
its proof that magic does exist
Deep within this human abyss

When mother nature comes to kiss
The ground and give it happiness
She warms the ground up from below
After she's covered us all in snow
Like humanity is in time out
And in the spring, mother lets us out.

With or Without You

Why're you coming at me
With lazy schemes and worn out scenes
Don't you know I've got big dreams

I've got no man to answer to

READ ME BiTCH (THiS iS WHAT iT MEANS TO BE HUMAN)

What makes you think I'll change for you

I'm trying make a future for myself
Not pay the bills for someone else

I need a man who comes to play and doesn't need me everyday
I need a man who understands how much this business really demands
I don't have time for childish games
Or dudes who don't even know my name
I've got better things to do
I can do them with

...or without you.

Organized Thoughts

I have to organize my thoughts
My heart is so fucking distraught
I can't even see that lining from here
It's dark and lonely and I'm full of fear
No money, can't work
My heart is so hurt
Humanity has nothing
It can eat dirt
I'm tired of this prideful dick
Who cannot believe I divorced him
A house note to pay
Roommate drunk every day
I don't see an honest way
Out of this mess
But I still have to keep my head
And take the high road instead.

Guilt Free Cake

It's enticing...
To think of cake with icing
Thick and rich inside my lips
And chocolate on my fingertips
The cherries pop with such sweet flavor
It's a taste I like to savor
As it rolls inside my mouth
It tastes so good, inside and out
I wonder what it really takes
To eat guilt free chocolate cake?

I Remember the Love

It's fresh cut grass and swings at the park
It's climbing trees and digging in dirt
It's fresh baked bread with melted butter
It's Christmas carols sung in the winter

And it's love
I remember love
I remember walks to the park
Before everything went dark
Life wasn't what it used to be
    ...and I wasn't ok with being me

But I do remember love
And long walks to get subs
And riding our bikes all around in circles
Writing at night, about our days, in our journals
And I miss those days
Before everything frayed

READ ME BiTCH (THiS iS WHAT iT MEANS TO BE HUMAN)

And I had to stay…

      away...

But there was love.
And long drives to the hub
Music blaring...me staring
Out of a window into the night
Thinking back on details of that last fight
Wondering if I was ok....yes i remember love

I remember love
I remember walks to the park
Before everything went dark
Life wasn't what it used to be
      …and I wasn't ok with being me.

Blurry Days

Blurry days are full of confusion
And not at all like blue ones
And not like donut and coffee days
Where all that's missing are the sun's warm rays

No, blurry days are full of pain
And nothing seems to go my way
But then I always choose to stay
....because I said I'd wait for you

The Fire

I don't like the way I feel
Like nothing that I thought was real
These things I guess I wanted to see
So I dreamt it all: make believe
Just like a stupid little girl
Pretending in a grown up world.

So why I felt safe I will never know
When your hand was on my throat
You held it there with total control
But I didn't know
...if you were gonna let go.

And then your grip got tighter
I began to feel a fire
Deep inside, that started to grow
And now I wonder if you feel the same
And...I'm curious if I'll ever know.

Walls

I want to be in love with you
But you won't let me fall
Everytime I turn around
...you put up a wall.

And I have walls so high
You can't see inside
And you don't seem to care

READ ME BiTCH (ThiS iS WHAT iT MEANS TO BE HUMAN)

That I let you in there
So I kicked you out
And now you scream and shout.

Now that I won't let you in
Even though you don't begin
To try and include me
I'm a well kept secret
No one else can see.

I wish I was in love with you
But you won't let me fall
Everytime I turn around
You put up a new wall.

Social Suicide

Social suicide
That's what it is
You let that shit rise
And fill you inside
And finally you say what's on your mind
And it's instant social suicide
Every single time
No matter what you say or do
It always comes back to you
Like a boomerang you threw
So maybe it's better if no one knew
Exactly what I said to you.

Narcissist

It's crazy how close the ground looks to the sky
Ribbons of green light dance in the night
And polar bears walk quietly by

And I think to myself about you and I
And my heart silently cries...
For a moment, then I remind

...myself that you were cold
That your heart to me was closed
...deep inside your being
You couldn't even reason

Nothing's more important than you
And that really is the reason we're through
Not because of something I did
Not because I constantly hid
Behind a wall of stone
That could not be overthrown...

    ...by you

Because you didn't even try

And now we say ~

    Good bye.

Good-Bye

I think this is the end
I won't go through it again
I can't do this anymore

READ ME BiTCH (THiS iS WHAT iT MEANS TO BE HUMAN)

Yes, I have to close that door
    *** *** ***
I've got to say goodbye
I hope you learn to fly
Learn to change when change is needed
See the warning…and learn to heed it.

Untitled

We all ask the question in some capacity
Is this endeavor worth our energy
Is it better than what we see
When we let things be?

Can it survive trials and tribulations?
Will it be humble and without trepidation?
There's no way to know if you don't try
And honestly if your arm reaches the sky

Chase the endeavor
We don't have forever
The sky's the limit
If your heart is in it

Fix Your Picker

You held on to something that never existed
No matter what you insisted
The truth of it was it was never a thing
No matter what you thought you could bring

You chose wrong when faced with that decision
Fix your picker...that's your mission

Figure a new way out to choose
A different kind of person
....with a new attitude...

And I Wonder…

My head is in the clouds
I float around from town to town
Set up the gear and I sing my song
Then i home and I toke on my bong
And I wonder if anyone heard what I said
If the message I wrote went over their heads
Or if time stood still
Broken words on window sills
Was life was treated with love again?
What if we don't hide in the sand?
Yeah, I wonder if anyone heard what I said?
Or if all of that meaning lay on the floor
                …dead.

Insomnia

Something doesn't feel right
You can't even sleep at night
Unsettled in your skin
Fear slowly creeping in
Feeling small and out of touch
You put a prayer up to above
And you slowly close your eyes
To be met with nightmares, what a surprise

READ ME BiTCH (THiS iS WHAT iT MEANS TO BE HUMAN)

Thoughts and Prayers

Humanity today
Is different from yesterday
It used to be that people cared about what you had to say
Now everyone wants something
And no one is giving
And that seems to make life really hard living
You did say you'd be there
And you were, no matter where
But when you asked for help
No one really cared
But they all said they'd send
all their thoughts and prayers.

Shady Motherfuckers

Shady motherfuckers creeping…sitting in the park
Shady motherfuckers sneaking round late after dark
Shady motherfuckers hiding wives inside their homes
Shady motherfuckers thinking they can bone
Shady motherfuckers keeping secrets they shouldn't keep
Trying lies and half-truths all up on their feeds

These shady motherfuckers ask for dates in parking lots
'Cuz these shady motherfuckers can't afford the coffee shop
Shady motherfuckers don't care what they get
Just as long as they get…their chance in your head

And shady motherfuckers lie
Tell you what you want to hear
Show you what you want to see…through a double sided mirror

Cash it in
Babe, it's all a show
Just let it go
Let that asshole know
He can't touch you anymore
Not since you shut that door
So really...who cares what he said
Don't let him have that space free in your head
Charge his ass for cold hard cash
Then treat yourself instead

Catch and Release (Intrusive Thoughts)
You can have it for a moment but at the end you let it go...
Because its life is valid and it will die if you don't...

The trees sing softly in gratitude…
 Thank you in a happy tune

But now you think, as you cross the bridge
Maybe you could not have let that fishy live.

Dreams
I dream about being kissed some nights
Then I wake up and wish it was my life
Then I'd be kissed all the time

I dream about hands and legs and twisted sheets
I wake up disappointed it was all a dream
Damn it, I just want to be kissed like that
Not wake up to wishing I could go back

READ ME BiTCH (THiS iS WHAT iT MEANS TO BE HUMAN)

Physical touch is so much on my mind
And now I think I need to find
Something else to dream about
Because these dreams make me scream out loud

Bliss

If I was to kiss someone's lips
While their hands gently gripped my hips
To pull me closer into that kiss
I think i'd be ok with it
If I'm honest I'd be lost within the confines of that bliss.

Maybe, it's Real

I don't know why
I have so much fear inside
And why i can't just resign
Myself to the way I feel
And accept that maybe this friend is real
He won't steal my money or my heart
And leave me broke down with a full cart.

Girl

Girl, don't start believing
Someone else's description
of your character
It's just vernacular
And the way they say it is so impractical
And how they portray you
You know...that way that they paint you

READ ME BiTCH (THiS iS WHAT iT MEANS TO BE HUMAN)

In a light that's different from what you desire
One that portrays you as kind of a climber
Or maybe just a slut
Oooo that one fucking cuts
Deep into your skin
It makes you feel like you hate him
All over again

You're dropping the deal
You stand there; then kneel
When the knife touches your skin
And then maybe you feel like you hate him and then

Girl...stop.
Breathe for a moment
This dude is gone-he's out of the donut
You don't have to worry if he never owns it
He's gonna say something everyday
And you know the way
That he tries to word play
And make them all think he's innocent
It doesn't matter, not even a minute

No one believes him
When he's all about it
If he was so great
Then you would've stayed
Lying on sheets made of satin

You'd be happy to let him be the captain
Of the world you created
But his sharp ass words left you empty and naked

READ ME BiTCH (THiS iS WHAT iT MEANS TO BE HUMAN)

And beaten on the floor
And girl, you don't need that shit anymore
You don't have to worry; you don't have to fear
When this is all done he will never come near

You've made new friends
This time it's the end
So stop lying in bed
And worrying at night
He isn't coming with a big sharp knife

His words are just words
And he ain't on the curve
So it doesn't matter if he tries to blurt
Personal matters
Let him chat his chatter

Let that shit fucking go
Who cares what he says
Don't let negativity fill up your head
He's out of your house and out of your bed

You're in a place where your dreams get fed
So what if sometimes
Some words get said?

You Instead
He has all of my attention
There's no competition
I simply cannot focus on you
Until I can get this other dude out of my fucking view
But...I don't really want to

READ ME BiTCH (THiS iS WHAT iT MEANS TO BE HUMAN)

I like the way it looks from here
No pressure, no worries, not that kind of atmosphere
I can breathe where i'm at
I'm not worried or fat
I'm sleeping at night and I'm eating alright
My mind is balanced and yet I'm still challenged in just the way I need to be
So, you see, I don't think you are the guy for me
You'd have to turn my head
And make me see you instead

Distrust

There are cracks within my walls
Some get bigger and others stay small
Some grow at a rapid rate
Faster than i can hesitate
I'm so afraid my walls will fall
And leave me feeling meek and small

But, I can feel you seeping in
Filling voids that might have been
Empty til the end of time
Replacing all my emptiness
And lighting up my mind.

Integrity

Who I am is hard to see
Because I hide behind the scenes
In the back I prefer to be
Then up in front

READ ME BiTCH (THiS iS WHAT iT MEANS TO BE HUMAN)

For all to see

And I watch people in the world
Sometimes I think of naughty girls
Sometimes I think of sweaty nights
And sometimes I think of starry skies

I dream of being free someday
Free from worry, free from pain
I want that house up on the hill
Where I can feel that breathy thrill
While music echoes off the walls
And I dance naked through the halls

I want a horse, some dogs, a pig
And a good man to share it with
I don't want a fast paced life
A different bed for every night

No, I want my flowers to grow
So I can sit and read and know
That even though this world is small
And there is no getting away from it all

I can still hide here and hear raindrops in my ears
And I'm small and insignificant
But when you look at how magnificent
The beauty of this world can be
When it's untouched by humanity

So, I have nothing profound to say
And I'm not special in any way
I don't have any fancy things

READ ME BiTCH (THiS iS WHAT iT MEANS TO BE HUMAN)

No jeweled bracelets or golden rings
Sarcasm runs inside my veins
And music flows inside my brain

I'm smart and mindful
True and heartfelt
I don't have time for any bullshit
So, if you want to talk to me
      …you'll have to speak with integrity…

Over

Boy, why are you coming at me like that?
Like you've got some kind of monkey clawing at your back.
Like you've got something to prove.
Naw dude, get the fuck back, just move.
Get out of my way, I ain't got time for your shit.
I'm moving on now and I gotta itch.

What you thought you knew.
What you wanted to do.
You can forget 'cuz now we're through.

I'm not that girl you thought I would be.
Wrapped up in your insanity.
Sometimes I surprise myself;
When I speak up about anything else.
Then what you think I should be.

I worked hard to get out of my funk.
And you dragged me back in...fucking slam dunk.
But no, no more.
Bro. I'm telling you, I'm out the door.

Forget about me, you don't know me no-more.

Don't call me,
don't text me,
don't try to come over,
I don't want to see you...

You are so last October.

In The Afterwards
There is so much damage...
Thoughts and feelings mismanaged...
Nothing for anyone to eat…
No leftover feelings to feed…
The hungry stares of those who see...
Me...
Alone in this room...
Wondering what the hell I should do...

If I can even find the path...
That puts me where I'll need to ask...
A few more questions down the road....

Find out things I need to know...
So I can be secure…
And know my voice is heard.

Petrichor

I love the rain...and the way it stains…
The ground beneath my feet…
Giving the earth a needed drink…

And I can smell the petrichor…
As it rises from the earth's damp floor…
Filling my nose with so much more…
Then I can even handle…
Memories flash like photos on a mantle…

So I set down my candle…
And look out into the night…
And watch the rain dance in the firelight…
The earth demands my attention tonight…
So, I opened the door…
    …and I let in the petrichor.

Secrets

The secrets inside me eat holes in my soul
Ripping and tearing deep into my bones
I can't speak them out for the words just won't come
At least not in a way that allows them to run

My secrets keep me inside and away
They keep me from saying things I want to say
I am frozen in place and locked into this space
FUCK YOU for leaving me here in this waste

Fuck you for giving me secrets i cant tell

READ ME BiTCH (THiS iS WHAT iT MEANS TO BE HUMAN)

For taking my innocence and ringing that bell
You lied and you stole, you put me in a cell
And then left me alone, afraid and unwell

I learned how to climb,
How to hold on and survive.
Even when it meant
I was fighting for my life

But these secrets I keep hold me hostage
I can't breathe or speak
…or eat;
      …only cry

These secrets can consume me
They crawl in through my seams
And seep out in disguises through cleverly marked dreams
They sneak in through windows, just to hear me scream

And I know…if I let go of
All these secrets, in time
I might just learn to defer that which isn't mine

Maybe I'll learn to bury them deep
Maybe one day I'll be able to sleep
But if I allow myself to replace
The dreams that always seem to give chase
How will I know…if my secrets escape?

Thoughtful Answers

So, I want to talk
And ask you many questions
With thoughtful answers.

I want to absorb
Your knowledge and understand
Your choices in life.

I believe magic
Exists to show us the way
We will overcome.

All these challenges
Create connections between us
We learn to include.

Those who may be lost
To some but not to others
We learn to adapt.

So, you see me now
And I want to talk to you
And ask you questions.

Yes, I want to talk
And ask you many questions
With thoughtful answers.

Nightmares

It's like a hot searing knife slicing deep in my skin
First it cuts deep and then it comes and cuts again

Penetrating my dreams in ways yet unseen
Creeping in the darkness...it waits for me
To run out in the street
Where it sits and it waits for me?

Cutting deep into my dreams
It solicits those screams it wishes to hear
It feeds on my fear
And I know that it's coming
I hear the blade humming
As it flashes through the air

And I run and im scared
Because I know that knife cuts deep
And I know that I will feel
The searing hot pain
Deep in my veins
As the tip of that knife cuts into my dreams
Causing them to bleed
All over my sheets

And I wake up in fear
How the hell did I get here?

The Trap

Time is such a funny beast
It ticks and tocks; locks things into place
it gives you the impression that we're in some kind of race.

READ ME BiTCH (THiS iS WHAT iT MEANS TO BE HUMAN)

But at the end of the day
There's nothing to say
Even if time decides to stray

In every possible way
It still somehow wins
Despite our victory grins

Should we already know
It doesn't matter how old
Or how cold we keep ourselves
…because in the end we don't save
Eventually, time whisks us all away

Music is the Only Thing

Music is the only thing
My attention brings
It holds me down when I have wings
Reminds me that I need to sing

Gives me something to meditate on
Gives me peace when I'm worn down
And sometimes when my spirit flies
Far off deep into the night

I can hear the mellow tones
Of music playing in my bones
Music brings me back to land
Sometimes it's my only friend

She follows me into tunnels

And stays when my thoughts are troubled
Music sits when I am sad
She sits with me and holds my hand

Younger Ways

Twinkling lights like dancing fairies
On the branches of those cherry trees
Reminded me of my yesterdays
Younger days and younger ways of perceiving the world around me

There is something in the air
Nostalgia rises with style and flair
Your face flashes before my eyes with memories
that rise and bring me to my knees
Reminding me of things long ago forgotten and lost on the breeze

And as I walk down all these roads again
I see the ghosts of my old friends as we laugh and sing and yell and then
Everything seems to have come to an end

I remember how I used to be
Working hard and always sad
I made money but I never had
Learning that my choices were bad
Was the best realization I've ever had

Funny how I see
A light shining through in a tree
And it brings such random memories

.....of younger days and younger ways

...Of perceiving the world around me.

Something I Said
Sometimes I speak up tall and then I step back
I think to myself, "I wish I hadn't said that"
i put myself out there for people to see
Then BOOM here's my old friend...anxiety
I want to hide in my room...shake off the doom
Sneak out my window...walk down to the flume
Maybe the kind of silence there
Will help me calm the air
Inside my head…whenever I say something I wish I hadn't said.

Lost Boy
On a park bench late one night.
You decided to take your own life.
You never called to ask for help.
Maybe you thought you were helping yourself?

You couldn't handle the world this way.
But you never had anything negative to say.
That didn't support your narrative.
If things were so good...why didn't you live?

Why didn't you call to let me know you were here?
I would've SO loved to see you, my dear.

I have these old pictures that will tatter and fade.
And never again will I feel your embrace.
I remember the first time I saw your tiny face.

And I'm filled with such sadness for all of the pain.
You must have felt sitting there in the rain.

    ...and wind and snow...

        That dark and lonely night

            When you chose to take
      your life.

The Burn
I want to feel the burn
I want my reward for the time I discern
Between feeling the fire
...and being drenched in cold water

I want to feel the sun
As it falls on my shoulders and keeps me warm
Not the winds as they blow through my clothes...all tattered and torn
I want the freedom of contentment without the tiresome shackles of resentment

I want to swim in warm clear waters
That allow me to see farther
Then I've seen before
Then I want to see more

I want to clearly see
What's in front of me
Before I reach the rocky shore

Yes, I want to feel that burn
And I want my reward for the time I discern
Between feeling that fire
...And being drenched in cold water.

Think Before You Act

though your heart screams at decibels unimagined...
Your mouth stays closed while your eyes remain open...
With your chin up, and your pride intact...
Stand tall, sweet friend.
Think before you act.

The Heart of June

Why did I let you stand in my way?
Like every single fucking day?
When could I have been at the river playing?
I let you lock me up inside this room?
Where my flowers never bloomed.
And you always said you're coming

              ...soon?

Damn...it always ends this way
Some dude who promises to stay
But then when he finally goes away

Maybe I don't want him back
Or maybe everything falls flat
And he doesn't even try the key
    …that he begged of me

I let you stand in my way
Its my fault that I let you stay
I'll have to explain away
The foolish way that my heart breaks
Everytime I think of you
Which should be easy

    …because I want out of this room
Where my flowers don't bloom
Not even in the hottest part of June.

Her Dream

Your eyes are deep like the ocean but open and searching and still hiding
so much from her as she searches for answers to
questions seeking to understand the human you became

Why, when she asked them…did you silence her
And leave her

When she found you
It was after a long journey over mountains and hills and seas.
She journeyed by train, by boat, bus and foot just to see your face.
To feel the heat of your body next to hers.

READ ME BiTCH (THiS iS WHAT iT MEANS TO BE HUMAN)

She traveled so far to find you

It was here; at the base of your porch that she marveled at the construction of your home
Crafted, she said, not built, a true masterpiece

As she wandered down a long hallway, searching...for you

She heard voices echoing against the walls that time had long ago forgotten...she wondered if she would be forgotten and then she continued on...wandering
Until she found you

Standing tall and confident on the other side of the glass
With your back turned

Like a statue.

Unrequited
Unrequited
Means: one-sided
Unseen or closed minded
A barren landscape
Like a cigarette left burning in the ashtray
Within these hostile dimensions
You hope for some kind of ascension
Or maybe just an answer to that age old question
But in the end it doesn't matter
truly it's all just mindless chatter
You keep hearing inside your head
Daydreams and wishes instead
Of seeing the fucking omen

READ ME BiTCH (THiS iS WHAT iT MEANS TO BE HUMAN)

There are no stolen moments
They do not exist
So please desist
From all your bullshit

This interest is one sided
Yes, I'm saying
Your love is unrequited

But still you try to make me see   **I am not undecided**
That you're the only one for me   **Your love is simply…**
Sorry friend, it just can't be   **Unrequited.**
There is no future in our dreams
There is no "our dreams"
This is all just fake

And I refuse to placate
There is no way that you can make

Me love you in that special way.

Stop driving by my house, it's creepy
Don't call upon your magic genie
He can't change my heart's desires
There is nothing that you can acquire
That will make me fall in love with you
Despite that picture that you drew.

Creepy, Night-time Sounds

Its different smells and night time sounds
That always seem to creep me out
When I'm stuck at someone's house
Like when my fucking lights go out

Twisting, twirling, falling snow
Lent the sky a purple glow
Snowflakes stacked up on the road
And I was careful, "in the zone"

But my car began to slide
And suddenly my life
Flashed before my eyes and i knew i couldn't drive
All the way to Kent that night...
I'd just stay home.
So, I called my friend, said "I'm not going"

But he said he'd come to get me.
Despite me asking differently
And now here I sit.
Without my shit
in someone else's house
With someone else's nighttime sounds
Creeping all around me

And in the darkness of this house

        That shit is really creepy.

The Nature of Death

Have you ever felt that empty hole
When you get to know a beautiful soul
A human that is so meaningful
That when they left this earth
You felt their worth
On such an intimate level
That you can't begin to back peddle.

You have to admit that you loved them and shit
Because really there's no way around it
And it hurts
Like it burns.

Deep into your bones
And it deafens your tones
That kind of hurt that won't leave you alone
it follows you home
Settles into the stone
it's a heavy sadness that won't leave you alone.

A sadness you learn to deal with
Because you damn sure never heal it
it's an ache you get used to but just like a child
You will never stop missing that bright shining smile
Or listening to the sound of their voice for a while.

You never get tired their mark
The one that they left here on this rock
where we all have to walk
and learn how to process the deepest of loss.

                         That kind of hole…

> Have you got that kind of
> hole deep inside your soul?

Reaching Out

No one is listening.
Its clear to me now as I sit here and bitch
And watch raindrops drip down
As they fall and then split by this porch, on the ground

Where I sit and I sift through my shit;
Fuck I'm tired of this

I am tired of sitting here all alone
With nothing to do but scroll through my phone
Why? When no one is listening can i not stop checking
To see if I'm connecting
With something out there
Do I really need someone to care?

Because no one is listening
There is no one there
When that realization finally becomes clear
In a way I can't help but to hear
Disappointment sets in
Because I'm alone again

And that feeling stays for way too long.

I'm tired of singing this same old song
I hate feeling like I don't count

READ ME BiTCH (THiS iS WHAT iT MEANS TO BE HUMAN)

I need to know that somehow i amount
… to be worth something…
A phone call or message or maybe some touching.

I've been alone for so fucking long
Writing too many songs about sadness prolonged
Sometimes I reach out through words
But my feelings get lost in the wind with the birds..
Expressing myself is so hard these days
When i feel like I have so much to say
...but no one is listening…

I guess I'll just sit here and watch the raindrops fall and glisten.

Waiting For Patience to Pay

The meaning of patience is torture
It's suffering
It is waiting for something that may not be coming
	…but it could...if you're patient and wait
Your greatest desire might come through that gate
   ~and give a sweet victory for you to taste

They say patience is a virtue
Something you should want too
But is virtue a paradise like Honolulu?

Because patience to me
Is like waiting for free
For things that most likely won't ever be
But still I sit there and I wait
Like hungry birds on the gate

Waiting for my desire to satiate
    ...I am waiting for patience to pay
        ...and I wonder
            ...exactly how long will this take?

Friendly Connection

That simple sense of friendly affection
it's indicative of connection
Or...some kind of ionic bond
That cannot be broken no matter the cause

When there's just a lonely song
And that ionic fucking bond
Be thankful that there is connection
Enjoy the friendly affection.

Sleep 𝓏𝓏 Evades Me

My eyes don't want to close…
Everytime I start to doze…
They open wide with fright…
Like maybe something's hiding tonight…
Like maybe something mean is sneaking…
Waiting for a chance to creep in…
And infect my dreams with nightmares…
Leave me open-eyed and scared…

And then I start to doze again…

READ ME BiTCH (THiS iS WHAT iT MEANS TO BE HUMAN)

But nightmares always come right in…
And color all my skies in shades red…
And then I wonder if I'm dead…
Sometimes there is so much shit I can't get off my mind…
It doesn't matter what I try…
But FUCK I need to get some sleep!
Monsters just stop bothering me!

it's so fucking late at night…
I wonder if I turn off the light if I'll be able to close my eyes?
And maybe...
Just maybe...
Will I get to sleep tonight?

Wild Woman

Old woman, why…
Why are you jiving there?
With braids in your hair
And flowers everywhere?
What are you even doing?

Your clothes obviously need sewing
And you don't seem to have any knowing
Of what's happening today
With the way you just sashay
Through this room
With a half moon
Smile on your face

READ ME BiTCH (THiS iS WHAT iT MEANS TO BE HUMAN)

Everyone is giving you space
And you are loving every second
You don't even care when security comes to reckon
With you and your dancing feet

I find you so sweet
In my wildest dreams
I hope I grow up to dance and sway
In worn out jeans
Without a care
And flowers in my hair
While security escorts me out of there

Smoke and Music Notes

I dreamt of you again last night
You quietly crept into my sleep
      So purposefully.

I knew it was you from the timbre of your voice
So similar to mine and you came so close
But still…
You were just out of reach

I dreamt of you last night
Like you were calling to me from the other side
As if you reached through time and space
To meet me here in this lonely place
To hold my hand; gently stroke my face
I could feel the warmth of your skin

READ ME BITCH (THIS IS WHAT IT MEANS TO BE HUMAN)

As if your heart began to beat again
And all those stories I heard of you
Had been untrue

Then you left me and i reached for you
My fingers grasping at ribbons of smoke
And music notes
That for a moment spoke the truth
Yes. I dreamt of you last night

Like you were calling to me from the other side
With a message to send
And before the end…they opened the door.

Heart Shaped Faces

Heart shaped faces fill lonely spaces built by cracks inside my walls
Cracks designed to make them fall
Deep cracks that run inside them all

These heart shaped faces in lonely spaces searching for human connection..
Are trying to make that human investment
They search for some kind of direction
They don't know what they're looking for
They reach out blindly; searching for more

Childlike innocence surrounds their base
As if they were newborns inside of this space
And they reach and they grab and embrace
What they grab onto in each single case

These heart shaped faces that can't find their path
And instead of looking they try to bask
Bask in light that's not theirs;
Take credit for others' airs
And make a stink when someone shares
Something they think isn't fair

Small and heart shaped faces
That leave small and heart shaped spaces
On pictures of pretty faces
That they never get to kiss
But somehow find a way to miss
I know the one for me won't have to look and leave
Little heart shaped signs on any simple words of mine
    …that I may have left behind
'Cuz I left different crumbs for him to find
Crumbs that take walls down from the inside

Big, Old Bones

Setting under these trees for so long
Big, Old Bones sing their song
To the forest and the trees
And, eventually, to me

They are posted up like a sentinel…
Bearing the frost and wind and the harshest breeze
    Yes, these bones have a story for me

Their strength and massive size are like a beacon in the night

READ ME BiTCH (THiS iS WHAT iT MEANS TO BE HUMAN)

For others to come and seek shelter
From all the helter skelter of the weather weathering outside

And so these creatures come and hide
…inside
                These big old bones
                Posted up by the riverside
                      Just waiting…

    Big old bones look like home to some
    To others it's a fearful thing
    The devil pulling his marionette strings
    Delivering. Fear. Confusion. Anger
    So much chaos in the face of danger
    But they are just big old bones on these rocky shores

        They don't look like much

But they are so much more

Shade from the hot sun

        A place to stay dry when the river runs

        A place to be warm

When the cold reaches deep into your core

And time stands still on those river shores
      Yes, these bones will be a home
        No matter who it is who happens to come

Until the sun shines bright again

        New life emerges and begins
                Big old bones that see so much

Through Nature's fury and her lust
        The different and new
        The colors and hues
    And how many times has an apology been due
    To those big old bones that stay
    Right there by the riverside day after day

                …Waiting for some small
                    creature…

                        …To need
                a place to stay.

Little Crumbs
I like the gray days best…
They have clouds that float like pillows and encourage us to rest
Those gentle wisps of clouds
As they reach down to touch the ground
Those wisps are beautiful

Little clasps
Hope clinging to the past
Reaching down
Until they surround
Shading us from the sun

Then disappear, in the atmosphere
Leaving small traces they were here
Little crumbs
Kind of like we do...leaving this life for the next one

Perception

You are transient, temporary, straight up fugitive status
With your pics of big money and your gold global outlook

You've got big means and big scenes fulfilling big dreams
But you spend all your time somewhere in between.

Damn I wish I could wait forever but I had a choice
It was my journey to endeavor
I wanted to savor a moment with you
But when that time came you didn't come through
And you lied to me bro, what you said wasn't true

Now you say you're sorry
Like you've got this crazy theory
But, it's really about perception so
What's the fucking question, bro?
        ...Thought you knew what i was about
           ...Now...just keep my name out your mouth

Little Keys

Those days passed in a haze
But they left
Memories behind
Like little keys for you to find

Little keys unlock the past
Doors that close way too damn fast
And life just seems like it's a wrap

Make sure you bide your time
There still is gold for you to find

Remember, what you came here for
Find your keys; unlock those doors
Put both your feet up on that floor
And then reach out 'cause you
      ...want more.

Scream

Let music notes drip
From your fingertips
Inside
The confines
Of my lacy blue panties

Pull your fingers through my hair
Give me tingles everywhere
Don't just stand and stare
At me... in my lacy blue panties
I'm waiting for you to up your ante

READ ME BiTCH (THiS iS WHAT iT MEANS TO BE HUMAN)

Though, i wonder if you can handle the fire
Of a woman who builds her own empire
Can you give me what I need
I'm insatiable you'll see

Push me up against a wall
Kiss me hard so I feel small
Fuck me in a way ill remember
Leave me with a burning ember
Like it was all a dream

But first, you need to make me *scream*

Mud Puddles

It's like drowning some days
And life is a stupified daze
Not looking at the bigger picture
Too stuck inside the lonely fixtures

Missing all the fun
Alone and feeling numb
Chase away the loneliness
Ending up a fat ass mess

Please don't let the whole world see
What's become of me

Messages in Bubbles

She whispers messages into bubbles
Words of encouragement to her own spirit
And sends them out into the world for someone else to hear it

These messages of misconstrued misfortunes
Tell stories of those who lived tortured
Stories of those that lost their keys
What they did to find their peace
What it was they really got
Where they ended up
And what they forgot

She whispers messages of false hopes and means
Ideas that came to her in dreams
Where she had seen the glow
From her attic window

It was a broken sign
On the side of the road
A brilliant beacon in the night
Holding her attention to the type
And not highlighting that little word...NO.

She whispered out a story she kept
About that one time love had crept
Up on her and lit a spark
One late night deep in some park
That later fanned into flame
Then became

READ ME BiTCH (THiS iS WHAT iT MEANS TO BE HUMAN)

Something not easily explained

She whispers her messages into bubbles
She floats them gently on the wind
Hoping they will fly away
Help her find that one, true friend

Now she knows her words fall flat
Hard against a tempered glass
Designed for keeping out
Anything that might be loud

But she still sends her message out
Words like leaves fly about
Then she grins

Pours herself a sip of gin

And starts the timer over again

    …And this time she puts her money on
  the zephyr wind to win

After-Thoughts

It was a big mistake
I never meant to fade away
But I couldn't back down
So I stood my ground
Still I lost the battle that night…
Though I tried with all my might
To stop and not go through with it
Something to tell me I'd be ok
But then came the day

And still no one seemed to care
Still no one was ever there
I found myself all on my own
My mind went deep into that zone

I just needed a friend to sit with me
Someone who could see me for me
instead of what I couldn't be

So, I walked and talked

…and talked
    …and walked

I found myself there, at that spot
And I sat down by the tree
Leaned back and set my soul free
But it was a big mistake
                …I never meant to fade away.

…my life i didn't mean to take.

Strong Ass Bitch

I am a strong ass bitch
And I can handle my shit
I can stand up tall
Despite being small
I land on my feet
No matter the fall
And I will prevail
I won't become stale
i can be on my own
Little me, all alone
With shit being thrown
All at my face
But don't you worry, now
Cuz I'll be ok
I don't need to be fixed
Cuz I'm a strong ass bitch
And I can definitely handle
    ...all my own shit.

Desire

I want to feel your lips touch mine
Steal my breath and fill up my mind
I want to feel your hands on my hips
I want to feel you sliding in
I want to feel your lips on my body
kissing me like you really want me
And I want to feel your breath on my skin
Then when we're done
    ...I want to do it again

The Circle

This life is such a merry go round
You leave your home but you're on the same ground
You run from all your childhood terrors
Hiding behind the largest mirrors
Exploding smoke bombs in your wake
Colorful rainbows overtake
And anyone who tries to follow
Finds those memories hard to swallow
Memories shoved to the back of the drawer
Forgotten until they spill to the floor
And as the tears roll down your face
And all the air inside escapes

Yes, who you were before the change
Is why it is you aren't the same
You aren't who you used to be
And while this knowledge brings relief

That circle? it comes back around
Rock after rock...it is the same ground
And you ask yourself
WHY are you standing in THiS place
When you've worked SO hard to get away?

Let the People Go

You have to let the people go.

READ ME BiTCH (THiS iS WHAT iT MEANS TO BE HUMAN)

It doesn't really matter what they do or do not know
Sometimes when your chest gets tight
And you can't sleep at all at night
Sometimes when those monsters fight their way into your dreams
Recreating vivid scenes
Sometimes it's just better
To sit down and write a letter
Explain some random thing
Make that thing set in
Then turn and walk away
And keep yourself a little safe

Today, I NEED to Write

Today, I need to write
Sit on my own and watch clouds roll by
Follow trails planes make in the skies
And dream about my future life

Write lyrics to songs inside my head
Then clean my kitchen and make my bed
Organize my space instead
...of thinking of lost things
All the sadness that loss brings

Leaving me with a weight inside
So all I can do is sit and cry
Then I dry my swollen eyes

But today is not about the loss
It's not about the fucking cost
It's not about the cloudy skies

READ ME BiTCH (THiS iS WHAT iT MEANS TO BE HUMAN)

It's not about my teary eyes
It's those words that reside
...deep inside my restless mind
Today, I need to write
             ...and run away tonight

The Tangible Flow

it's a slow tingle that starts in my toes
And moves through my body in a tangible flow
Lighting up spaces I thought long lost
But that slow zing was the key to unlock
All of my hidden doors
And now I only want more
I want to feel that tangible flow
Start in my head and move to my toes

Profound

I wish I had something profound to say
But my mind is tired of thinking today
My eyes won't close despite the time
My thoughts won't quiet inside my mind

So I look for some distraction

inhuman, cold and waxen

Something to soften tumultuous thoughts
To help me bury my something lost
But I don't know how to play that game

READ ME BiTCH (THiS iS WHAT iT MEANS TO BE HUMAN)

So I wait my turn; til i hear my name

And then
I have nothing profound to say.
'Cuz my mind is tired of thinking today

I Wish

I wish I could call the otherside
'Cause sometimes I just need your advice
I need to hear your gentle voice
While you listen to my empty void
Man, I miss your face
And the way you occupied your space
And I miss the way we friended
I wish all that hadn't ended
I wish I could see you fly
Damn, I wish you hadn't died

Legacy

We are her legacy
We are what life was meant to be
The endless circle turning
Like restless ocean waters churning

She passed down all her stories
About her days in sun and glory
Her knowledge of the farm
And how to keep us safe from harm

READ ME BiTCH (THiS iS WHAT iT MEANS TO BE HUMAN)

She taught us how to be human
How to see that trouble is brewing

We are her legacy

We are what life was meant to be
that endless circle turning
Like restless ocean waters churning

She felt all our growing pains
As life continuously changed
Phones went in our pockets

And we talk, out loud, to light sockets

But she longs for the old ways

And the old days

And she prays
For peace to come in waves

Because we are her legacy
We are what life is meant to be
The endless circle turning
Like restless ocean waters churning

*We **are** her legacy.*

Fuck You and ALL You Do

Fuck you and all you do
I don't need another dude

READ ME BITCH (THIS IS WHAT IT MEANS TO BE HUMAN)

I need peace inside my head
But i'm waging war inside instead

I need to calm my nerves
Get me some good green herbs
Stop the madness where it starts
And no you cannot play the part

I know it's sad but, babe, it's true
You didn't even try to prove
Your fucking worth to me
So now, your ass can let me be
Yeah fuck you and all you do
I'm done with this...its fucking through.

Walk Away (The End)
I think I have to walk away
I think there's nothing left to say

I think that time has come and gone
I think we choose to not move on

So here we are...in a stagnant room
with air so thick we need a broom

To sweep up the misfortune
That let us down and left us tortured

By emotions out of our control
And thoughts we hid inside our souls

And...I'm sorry for what I did to you.
And I hope that you forgive me soon.

(***Credits***)

Do you ever wonder what comes after?
When the emptiness echoes with ghostly laughter?
After all the life is lived...
After the last kiss is kissed...
After all the time is spent...
And we've all faced our consequence...
Do we get a chance to rest?
Or do we face another test?
Will we get to chill and sit or have we not seen the hardest yet?
I often wonder what comes next...
After we face that consequence...
I wonder if I'll find my peace...
Will my thoughts slow down?
My mind released?
I, often, wonder what comes after...
When the emptiness fills with ghostly laughter...

Buck McCoy and Meghanne Storey Performing at a loca Seattle Brewery: Bad Jimmy's Brewing Company.

The Meghanne Storey Project
#AndBuck
At the Spanish Ballroom in Tacoma, Wa

READ ME BiTCH (THiS iS WHAT iT MEANS TO BE HUMAN)

Meghanne Storey

Meghanne Storey

READ ME BiTCH (THiS iS WHAT iT MEANS TO BE HUMAN)

Lamppost Magic

Meghanne Storey

#AndBuck

READ ME BiTCH (THiS iS WHAT iT MEANS TO BE HUMAN)

84

READ ME BiTCH (THiS iS WHAT iT MEANS TO BE HUMAN)

READ ME BiTCH (THiS iS WHAT iT MEANS TO BE HUMAN)

READ ME BiTCH (THiS iS WHAT iT MEANS TO BE HUMAN)

READ ME BiTCH (THiS iS WHAT iT MEANS TO BE HUMAN)

Made in the USA
Middletown, DE
13 December 2023

44604078R00054